SCIENCE OF THE SUMMER OLYMPICS

EDGE BOOKS

THE SCIENCE BEHIND TRACK AND FIELD

by Lisa J. Amstutz

Consultant:

Mark Walsh
Associate Professor of Exercise Science
Miami University
Oxford, OH

CAPSTONE PRESS
a capstone imprint

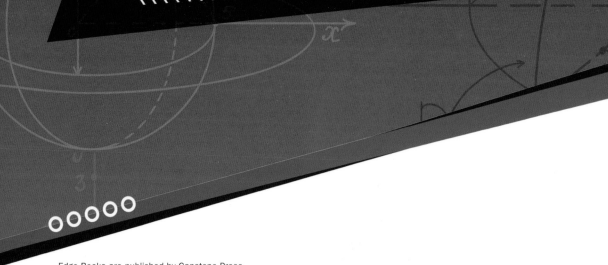

Edge Books are published by Capstone Press,
1710 Roe Crest Drive, North Mankato, Minnesota 56003
www.mycapstone.com

Library of Congress Cataloging-in-Publication Data
Cataloging-in-publication information is on file with the Library of Congress.

ISBN 978-1-4914-8158-5 (library binding)
ISBN 978-1-4914-8162-2 (paperback)
ISBN 978-1-4914-8166-0 (ebook pdf)

Editorial Credits
Arnold Ringstad, editor
Craig Hinton, designer and production specialist

Photo Credits
AP Images: 21 (top), David Davies/Press Association, 16, David J. Phillip, 1, 6–7, 29, Hassan Ammar, 22,
Kyodo, 27, Lefteris Pitarakis, 12–13, Mark Baker, 14–15, Matt Dunham, cover, 4, 19, 24, Mike Groll, 8, Pawel
Kopczynski, 26; Dorling Kindersley, 23; Dorling Kindersley/Thinkstock, 4–5, 18–19, 21 (bottom); Red Line
Editorial, 10–11, 28; pictorico/iStockphoto, 11

Printed in the United States of America in North Mankato, Minnesota
102015   2015CAP

TABLE OF CONTENTS

Jamaica's Usain Bolt dashes toward victory in the 100-meter sprint at the 2012 London Olympics.

long jump/ triple jump

TRACK AND FIELD
ARENA ⭕⭕⭕⭕⭕

hammer throw

discus

CHAPTER 1

GOING FOR
THE GOLD

Heads down and feet on the starting blocks, the runners wait. Bang! The starting pistol fires, and they're off. Arms and legs pumping, they race for the finish line with a single goal in mind: an Olympic medal. Who will be the next champion?

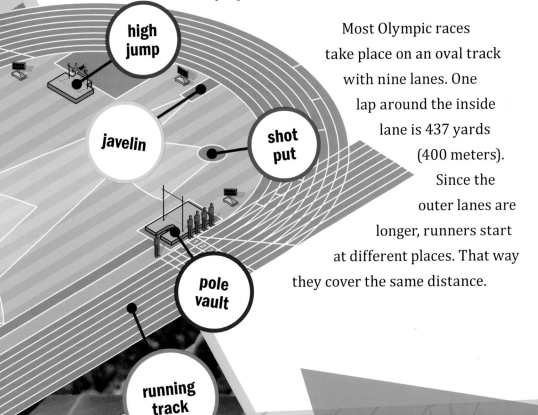

high jump

javelin

shot put

pole vault

running track

Most Olympic races take place on an oval track with nine lanes. One lap around the inside lane is 437 yards (400 meters). Since the outer lanes are longer, runners start at different places. That way they cover the same distance.

FIGHTING FORCES

drag

In the javelin throw, the force of an athlete's throw is working against two naturally occurring forces. The first is drag, or air resistance. As the javelin flies, it collides with air molecules. The collective force of these collisions slows down the javelin. The second force is gravity. Gravity attracts objects with mass toward each other. Since Earth is so much larger than the javelin, this force is only noticed in one direction. The javelin is pulled toward the center of the planet.

gravity

Jumping and throwing events are held on a large field inside the track. The field is covered with grass or artificial turf. Long jumpers land in a sandpit. High jumpers and pole-vaulters land in mats filled with soft padding, known as pits.

The Science of Track and Field

Great track and field athletes make their sports look easy. But nothing could be further from the truth. They train hard and make every motion count. They use their knowledge of physics to their advantage, working with **drag**, **gravity**, and **momentum**. Understanding the science of the sport can shave seconds off a racer's time. It can give a discus thrower the extra inch needed to win.

drag—the force that slows an object in motion traveling in air or water
gravity—a force that causes objects to move toward Earth's center
momentum—the mass of an object multiplied by its speed

Uganda's Stephen Kiprotich won the gold medal in the 26.2-mile (42.2-km) men's marathon race at the 2012 London Olympics.

CHAPTER 2

RUN LIKE
THE WIND

The world's fastest runners compete at the Summer Olympics every four years. They walk or run races ranging from 109 yards (100 m) to 31 miles (50 kilometers).

Drag is the force that slows these athletes the most. Air may look like empty space. But it is filled with countless molecules of invisible gas. The result of running into these molecules is drag. Sprinters wear tight clothing to reduce the amount of surface area struck by the air as they move. This lets them move faster.

What about Wind?

Have you ever tried to run on a windy day? The wind can push you along or slow you. Wind affects Olympic runners in the same way. It can increase or decrease the amount of drag. A runner's time does not count as a world record if a wind stronger than 6.6 feet (2 m) per second is blowing at her back. Too much wind gives a runner an unfair advantage.

On the Fast Track

At the 2012 London Olympics, Usain Bolt defended his gold medal in the 100-meter sprint. He ran the distance in 9.63 seconds, an Olympic record. The biomechanics of Bolt's sprinting give him an edge over his competitors. At 6 feet, 5 inches (1.96 m), he stands taller than the typical sprinter, giving him a long stride length. Most sprinters take 44 steps to complete the 100-meter race, but Bolt uses only 41.

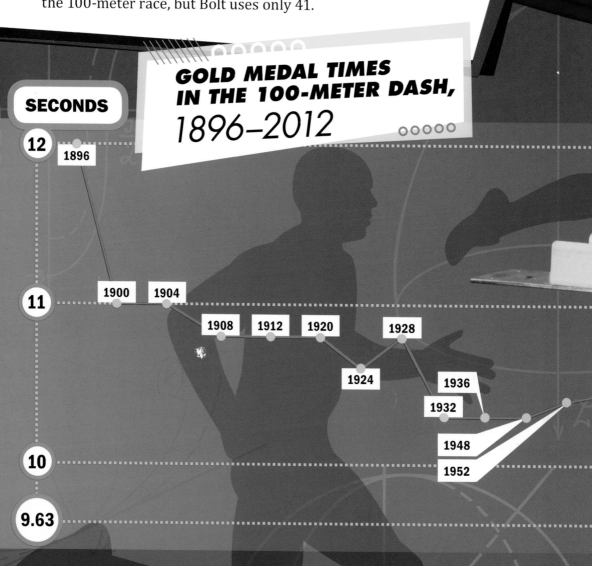

GOLD MEDAL TIMES IN THE 100-METER DASH, 1896–2012

SECONDS

12 — 1896

11 — 1900 — 1904 — 1908 — 1912 — 1920 — 1928 — 1924 — 1932 — 1936 — 1948 — 1952

10

9.63

Sprinters need a burst of power to speed up quickly. They place their feet against starting blocks and push off. Sir Isaac Newton's third law of motion says that for every action there is an equal and opposite reaction. The block does not move when a sprinter pushes on it. So the force from the sprinter's foot pushes against his body instead. This propels him forward at the start of the race and helps him reach his top speed as soon as possible.

The action of a sprinter's push against the starting block causes a reaction that accelerates the runner forward.

1956

1960

1964

1980

1972

1976

1968

1984

1992

1988

2000

1996

2004

2008

2012

9.63
Olympic record

In racewalking, competitors must have one foot touching the ground at all times.

Going the Distance

Can you imagine running 26.2 miles (42.2 km) without stopping? That's exactly what marathon runners do. The marathon is the longest Olympic running event. Racewalkers cover even more ground in the 50-kilometer racewalk.

Distance runners use energy differently than sprinters do. They do not move as fast, but they must go much farther. They train for **endurance** as well as speed.

Even the muscles of sprinters and distance runners differ. Fast-twitch muscle fibers move fast. They also get tired fast. Slow-twitch fibers react more slowly. But they can keep going much longer. Sprinters have more fast-twitch fibers in their muscles. Marathon runners have more slow-twitch fibers.

Distance runners try to save energy when they can. One way is by **drafting**. The first runner pushes air out of the way. The second runner has less air to push against. He conserves energy because there is less drag to fight.

endurance—the ability to remain active for a long time
draft—to run close behind another runner to lessen air resistance

13

Winning the Race

The end of the race is near, and the finish line in sight. The sprinters flash by in a blur. The race is too close to call. Luckily, high-tech finish line cameras can determine the winner.

These cameras turn on the instant the starting pistol fires. They connect to a laser beam at the finish line. When a runner crosses the beam, the cameras capture the moment. They record thousands of frames per second. If the race is close, officials can replay the ending frame by frame to see who won.

Distance events like the marathon do not use laser beams. Instead, runners wear special tags on their shoes. A mat at the starting line picks up the tag's signal. Mats every 3.1 miles (5 km) track the runners' progress. A mat at the finish line records each runner's final time.

Lasers and cameras help ensure medals are correctly awarded in close finishes.

Keeping Cool

When an athlete's muscles burn energy, they create lots of heat. The body needs to cool itself down—but how?

One trick is to send more blood to the skin. The outside air cools the blood before it flows back through the body. Another solution is sweat. Sweat is a liquid made by glands in the skin. It consists of water and small amounts of minerals, including sodium, potassium, and calcium. When the sweat **evaporates** into the air, it takes heat with it. Marathon runners may sweat a whole gallon (3.8 liters) of water during a race. They must drink a lot to replace the water they lose.

evaporate—to change from a liquid into a vapor

British athlete Greg Rutherford leaped to a gold-medal finish in the long jump in the 2012 London Olympics.

CHAPTER 3

ONE GIANT LEAP

Could you jump the length of two cars? Or leap over a stop sign? An Olympic jumper could!

To make their jaw-dropping leaps, athletes must fight the downward force of gravity. Every object has a **center of gravity**. This is the point where it would balance if you hung it from a string. When a person is standing still, his or her center of gravity is close to the navel. The center of gravity shifts as the body position changes. Olympic jumpers have to control their centers of gravity when they jump. By moving their arms and legs to adjust their centers of gravity, top athletes can jump higher and farther in their quests for medal-winning performances.

center of gravity—the point at which an object's weight is centered

Center
of gravity

A Running Jump

Long jumpers and triple jumpers sprint down
a 131-foot (40-m) track to gain speed. Then they
leap into a sand pit. Their running speed gives them
momentum. Even after their feet leave the ground, this
momentum carries them forward in the air. The faster
athletes run, the more momentum they have, and the
farther they can jump. This is why many athletes do well at
both sprinting and jumping events.

Once in the air, a long jumper swings her legs up
and forward. This pulls her center of gravity forward. The
forward and upward movement of her legs allow her to
reach a longer distance. She travels farther before touching
the sand. The jump is measured to the mark she made
in the sand while landing.

CENTER OF GRAVITY ○○○○○

American athlete Janay DeLoach Soukup stretches out her legs for landing in the long jump final during the 2012 London Olympics.

Jumping High

High jumpers must run and throw their bodies over a bar. The bar moves up each round. The last remaining jumper wins. The men's world record is just over 8 feet (2.44 m). The women's record is 6 feet, 10 inches (2.08 m).

The athlete has to raise his center of gravity as high as possible. After a short run, he launches himself into the air. Jumpers once leaped over the bar facedown. But in the 1960s, an American college athlete named Dick Fosbury had a better idea. He twisted his body while jumping to go over the bar faceup. It allowed him to clear higher bars without raising his center of gravity higher. It also made it less likely that an elbow or knee would bump the bar. Fosbury took home the gold medal at the 1968 Mexico City Olympics. This method is now known as the Fosbury Flop.

Dick Fosbury set a new record at the 1968 Mexico City Olympics using his revolutionary high-jump technique.

THE FOSBURY FLOP

High jumpers run toward the bar, then turn to leap over it faceup and backward. This technique is called the Fosbury Flop.

Acrobatic Athletes

The highest jumpers of all are the pole-vaulters. Imagine jumping over a giraffe. That's how high these athletes soar! They vault over a bar using a long pole made of fiberglass and carbon fiber. These materials are strong but flexible. They quickly spring back after they bend.

Pole-vaulters use two different kinds of energy in their jumps: **kinetic energy** and **potential energy**. Kinetic energy is the energy of motion. Potential energy is stored energy.

An enormous amount of energy is stored in the pole as it bends.

kinetic energy—the energy of motion
potential energy—stored energy

The pole stores energy briefly, then transfers it back to the athlete as it moves him over the crossbar.

The vaulter sprints down a 131-foot (40-m) track called a runway. This creates kinetic energy. She slams the pole into a small box. The vaulter's energy transfers to the bending pole as potential energy. As the pole straightens, it changes back into kinetic energy. It pushes the vaulter up and over the bar.

The vaulter drives her feet toward the sky, lifting her center of gravity as high as possible. At the top of the bar, she is upside down. She swings her feet over the bar and pushes the pole away. If all goes well, she lands on her back on the soft mat below.

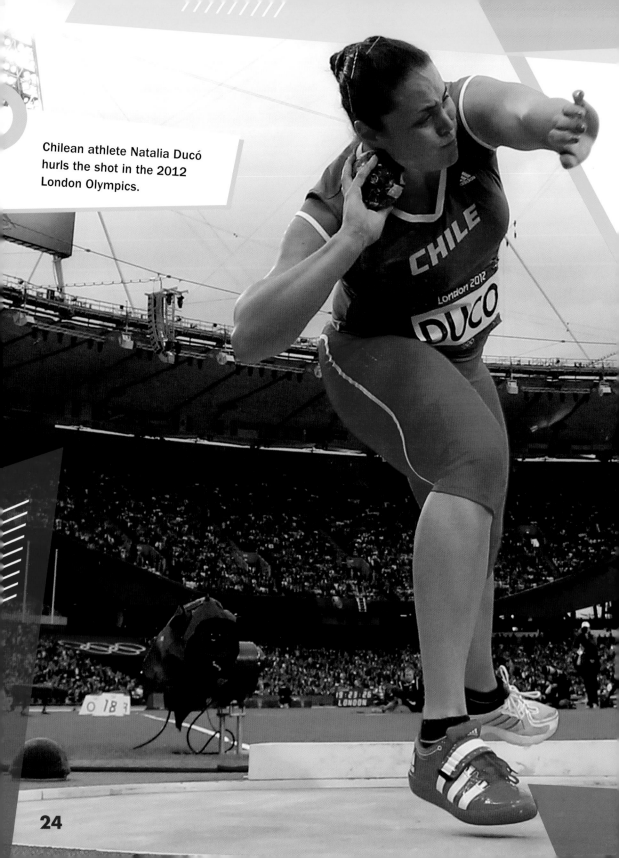

Chilean athlete Natalia Ducó hurls the shot in the 2012 London Olympics.

CHAPTER 4

THROWING
COMPETITIONS

People have been throwing stones for thousands of years. The Ancient Greeks held rock-throwing contests. Soldiers in the Middle Ages tossed cannonballs. Today, Olympians hurl lead balls the size of grapefruits. These are called shots. A shot weighs 8.8 pounds (4 kilograms) for women and 16 pounds (7.3 kg) for men. It takes great strength and skill to push this heavy weight through the air.

Shot-putters must stay inside a circle that is 7 feet (2.1 m) across. They spin around, making either a half turn or one and a half turns, depending on their chosen technique. During the spin, the athletes exert **centripetal force** to prevent the rotation from carrying the shot away. Then, they release the shot. The distance is determined by the speed of rotation, which gives momentum to the ball, and the shot-putter's arm muscles, which add power to the motion.

centripetal force—a force that holds an object along a curved path

Hammer It Home

The hammer throwing event involves a ball that is hooked to a cable. This "hammer" weighs the same as a shot. But it goes up to four times farther. How can this be?

The secret is the length of the cable. It lets the ball move in a larger circle than the shot does. The ball builds up more speed by the time it is released. The extra speed gives it more momentum and allows it to travel farther. When the athlete releases the cable, the hammer travels in an arc from the point of release.

China's Zhang Wenxiu prepares to release in the hammer throw event in the 2012 London Olympics.

Throwing Spears

Javelin throwers heave long, pointed sticks down the field. The thrower takes a running start to build momentum. When she stops, the energy travels up through her body and into the javelin. An extra push from her arm muscles makes it fly even farther.

Japanese athlete Genki Dean makes a throw in the javelin finals at the 2012 London Olympics.

Flying Saucers

The discus looks a bit like a Frisbee, but you wouldn't want to try catching one! This flat saucer is made of wood, rubber, or plastic with a metal rim. The men's discus weighs 4.4 pounds (2 kg). The women's is smaller and lighter at 2.2 pounds (1 kg).

The discus flies straight out from the point where it is released. The flat disk cuts through the air. Its shape helps it stay aloft, like an airplane wing. The air moves faster over the discus than under it. This causes a difference in air pressure that lifts the discus and helps it stay in the air.

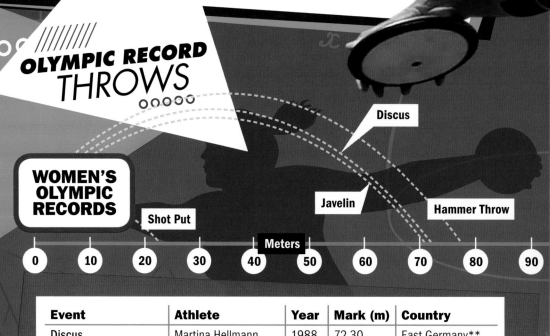

OLYMPIC RECORD THROWS

WOMEN'S OLYMPIC RECORDS

Discus

Javelin

Hammer Throw

Shot Put

Meters

0   10   20   30   40   50   60   70   80   90

Event	Athlete	Year	Mark (m)	Country
Discus	Martina Hellmann	1988	72.30	East Germany**
Hammer Throw	Tatyana Lysenko	2012	78.18	Russia
Javelin	Osleidys Menéndez	2004	71.53	Cuba
Shot Put	Ilona Slupianek	1980	22.41	East Germany**

*The Soviet Union split into several countries in 1991, including Russia.
**Germany split into East and West Germany in 1949. They joined together again to form modern Germany in 1990.

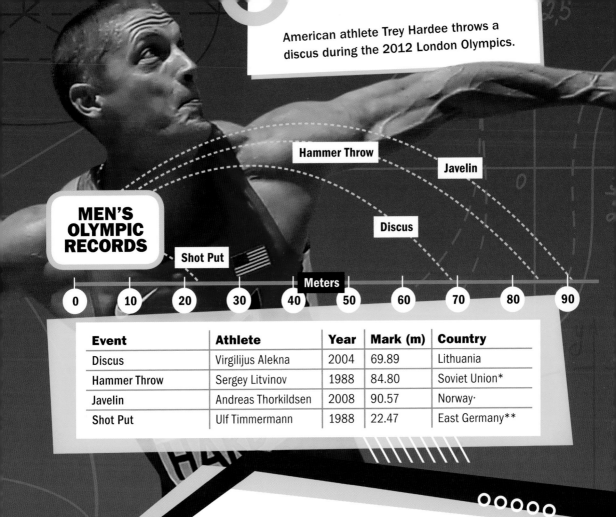

American athlete Trey Hardee throws a discus during the 2012 London Olympics.

MEN'S OLYMPIC RECORDS

Hammer Throw

Javelin

Discus

Shot Put

Meters

0   10   20   30   40   50   60   70   80   90

Event	Athlete	Year	Mark (m)	Country
Discus	Virgilijus Alekna	2004	69.89	Lithuania
Hammer Throw	Sergey Litvinov	1988	84.80	Soviet Union*
Javelin	Andreas Thorkildsen	2008	90.57	Norway·
Shot Put	Ulf Timmermann	1988	22.47	East Germany**

Always Advancing

Today scientists study what an athlete should eat to perform well. They research the best ways to move and to practice. They keep making better shoes and faster tracks. Athletes learn how to take advantage of the laws of physics to increase their distances and cut their finishing times.

Is there a limit to how fast humans can run, how high they can jump, and how far they can throw? No one really knows. But advances in science, technology, and talent are sure to keep bringing new Olympic records.

GLOSSARY

center of gravity (SEN-tur UHV GRAV-uh-tee)—the point at which an object's weight is centered

centripetal force (sen-TRI-puh-tul FORSS)—a force that holds an object along a curved path

draft (DRAFT)—to run close behind another runner to lessen air resistance

drag (DRAG)—the force that slows an object in motion traveling in air or water

endurance (en-DUR-ance)—the ability to remain active for a long time

evaporate (e-VAP-uh-rate)—to change from a liquid into a vapor

gravity (GRAV-uh-tee)—a force that causes objects to move toward Earth's center

kinetic energy (ki-NET-ik EN-ur-jee)—the energy of motion

momentum (moh-MEN-tuhm)—the mass of an object multiplied by its speed

potential energy (puh-TEN-shuhl EN-ur-jee)—stored energy

READ MORE

Gifford, Clive. *The Inside Story of Track and Field*. New York: Rosen Central, 2012.

Hunter, Nick. *High-Tech Olympics*. Chicago: Heinemann Library, 2012.

Johnson, Robin. *Take Off Track and Field*. New York: Crabtree Publishing Company, 2013.

CRITICAL THINKING USING THE COMMON CORE

1. Study the graphs on pages 28–29. Which thrown objects traveled the farthest? Why? How do the factors of gravity and air resistance come into play? (Integration of Knowledge and Ideas)

2. The graph on pages 10–11 shows how race times have gotten faster over the past century. The laws of physics that affect runners, such as air resistance and gravity, have not changed. What factors may have led to these decreased times? (Integration of Knowledge and Ideas)

INTERNET SITES

FactHound offers a safe, fun way to find Internet sites related to this book. All of the sites on FactHound have been researched by our staff.

Visit *www.facthound.com*

Type in this code: 9781491481585

Super-cool stuff!

Check out projects, games and lots more at
www.capstonekids.com

INDEX

30